THE STORY OF

ABRAHAM LINCOLN,
President for the People

THE STORY OF

ABRAHAM LINCOLN,
President for the People

BY LARRY WEINBERG

ILLUSTRATED BY TOM LaPADULA

A YEARLING BOOK

ABOUT THIS BOOK

The events described in this book are true. They have been carefully researched and excerpted from authentic autobiographies, writings, and commentaries. No part of this biography has been fictionalized. To learn more about Abraham Lincoln, ask your librarian to recommend other fine books you might read.

Published by
Dell Publishing
a division of
Bantam Doubleday Dell Publishing Group, Inc.
666 Fifth Avenue
New York, New York 10103

ISBN: 0-440-40411-8

Published by arrangement with Parachute Press, Inc.
Printed in the United States of America
February 1991
10 9 8 7 6 5 4 3 2 1
OPM

Dedicated to my beautiful Janie

Contents

Frontier Boy

We've all heard of the Abraham Lincoln, who became the sixteenth President of the United States. But his story begins with another Abraham Lincoln who lived and died before the great President was born. The first Abraham Lincoln, the President's grandfather, fought in the Revolutionary War and later on became a friend of the famous frontiersman Daniel Boone. Year after year Boone told him wonderful stories of the deep forests and bluegrass and rich black soil in Kentucky. Finally the first Abraham Lincoln sold his farm in Virginia and set off with his family across the Cumberland Gap.

The wilderness was the ancient hunting ground of the Iroquois, the Cherokee, and other Native American tribes. The Indians feared being pushed out of the forests again as they had been back East. Already the white men were cutting down wide patches of trees where the bear, wild turkey, and deer used to roam. And even worse, they were fencing in the land that had once belonged to all.

One day Abraham Lincoln put up a rail fence of his own. Suddenly there was the crack of a rifle. Lincoln's three sons were with him in the newly cleared field. When their father fell, the two older boys sprang into action. One headed for the nearby fort to get help; the other raced into the cabin for a weapon. But six-year-old Tom Lincoln didn't run. He bent down over his father's body. Young Tom didn't see the Indian come out of hiding until the man was standing over him.

There are some who say that the man picked up the boy and started to hurry off with him. Whether he meant to kill little Tom or take him to his tribe, no one knows. But suddenly another rifle spoke. The shot came from a musket Tom's brother Mordecai had poked out of a chink in the cabin wall. Mordecai had aimed at the shining silver ornament that hung from the brave's neck and hit it dead center. When the bullet struck, the badly wounded Indian threw up his arms, and Tom fell to the ground. Then the Indian staggered off into the thick woods.

Tom Lincoln grew up fatherless on the Kentucky frontier, near the banks of the Licking River. But he had family and friends. All his life he knew a girl called Nancy Hanks. As small children, they had traveled west in the same caravan of covered wagons.

Tom married Nancy one fine June day. At the wedding party the guests ate bear meat and wild turkey and popped lumps of maple sugar in their mouths while they drank coffee. Afterward, the young couple rode off on a horse to a cabin in the woods to start a little farm of their own.

The next year Nancy gave birth to Sarah Lincoln. Two years later, on February 12, 1809,

Nancy was about to give birth once again. Since there weren't any doctors in the area, Tom Lincoln went to fetch a neighbor whom people called the Granny Woman, although she was only twenty years old. She returned to the log cabin with Tom and delivered a brother for Sarah. Tom Lincoln, who had never forgotten the father who died at his feet when he was just a little boy, named the child Abraham.

The cabin they lived in was very small. It had just one window and a door that was tied on to the wall by strips of leather. There was no wood on the floor, just dirt that had been packed down hard.

Abe's father could have built a wooden floor if he'd had the time, for he was good at making things. In fact, Tom Lincoln liked carpentry much better than farming. That was the sort of work he had done before he got married and settled down in one place to raise a family. Now and then he still got jobs helping to build a church or a jail or someone else's cabin. But farming his own little piece of land took most of his time. And whenever he did have a chance to take a few hours just for himself, he'd pick up

4

his long rifle and go hunting. Hunting was Tom Lincoln's favorite pastime.

Still, the tiny cabin with its clay chimney was snug, even in the winter. And Nancy Lincoln kept her home a pleasant place. She sang the songs she had learned as a girl to her infant boy and his two-year-old sister, Sarah, while she cooked, mended, spun, and wove.

But Tom Lincoln wasn't doing very well on that farm. When Abe was two, the family moved to another piece of land ten miles away on Knob Creek. Abe would watch his "pappy" at work on the new farm, and he wanted to help. At planting time in the spring he followed his father, dropping pumpkin seeds between rows of corn.

When Abe grew a little bigger, he was allowed to sit bareback on the big horse while it was pulling the plow. But when Abe pleaded to go hunting with his pappy, he was told he was too young. Abe had to settle for chasing groundhogs and rabbits with his friend Austin.

One day when he and his friend grew hot and sweaty from running around, they tossed their caps on the ground. Austin stretched out under a tree, while Abe climbed up on a branch. Abe waited until Austin's eyes were closed. Then he plucked a ripe piece of fruit from the tree and dropped it on the upturned coonskin cap lying next to Austin's head. When it landed, yellow mush splattered everywhere.

Abe couldn't understand the grin on Austin's face until he climbed down from the tree. His friend had guessed what he was up to and switched hats. It was Abe's own cap that was smeared with mushed fruit!

But the day came when Abe was glad that Austin was a quick-witted boy. The two of them had gone down to Knob Creek to search for partridges. Abe remembered having seen them nesting on the other side of the creek. But the creek was swollen with rushing water and too wide for them to jump over. Noticing a narrow log that was lying across the water, Abe suggested that they pretend to be raccoons and crawl across on all fours to the far bank. Austin went first and crawled to the far bank. But Abe became frightened halfway across. Trembling, he lost his balance and fell into the stream. Aus-

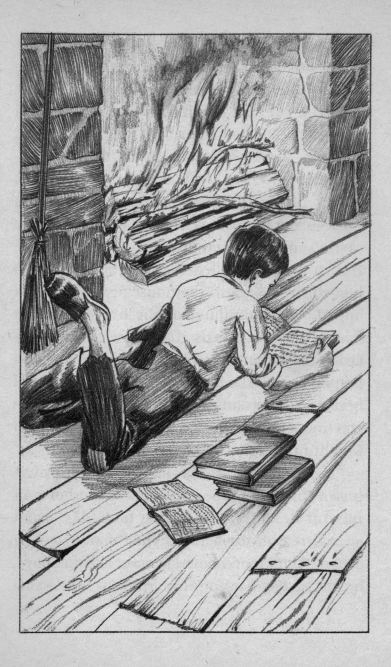

tin saw him go under, but like Abe, he didn't know how to swim. Suddenly he grabbed a long piece of wood from the ground and shoved one end of it into the water. He swung it around until Abe grabbed hold of it, then he pulled Abe out. Austin had saved Abe's life!

Often Abe was too busy to play. There was always plenty of work to do on the Lincoln farm—even for a six-year-old. He and his sister carried empty buckets down to the spring a mile from the house, filled them with water, then lugged them back to the house again. He went out to collect kindling for the fire. He used a hoe to dig out weeds that were choking the crops his father had planted. Abe and Sarah helped to feed the family by collecting nuts and berries in the woods. And almost as soon as Abe was big enough to lift an ax, Tom Lincoln taught him how to chop wood.

Abe's pappy would have kept him even busier, but when he was seven his mother sent him off to school for the first time. Abe had a special reason for being excited about starting school. Until then he had been a "shirttail boy," a youngster whose only clothing in warm weather was a shirt that hung down to his knees. Abe didn't like being dressed this way, especially since he was tall for his age. Some youngsters who were already wearing buckskin pants or jeans teased him about his shirt. One day, when he was on his way to the mill with corn to be ground into flour, he wrestled with several boys at the same time for making fun of him. But Abe's big embarrassment ended when he started school. The schoolmaster had made a rule. No boy would be admitted to his classroom who wasn't wearing a pair of britches!

The first schoolhouse Abe attended with his sister was an old abandoned cabin. People called it a "blab" school because all the children recited their lessons aloud at the same time. It would have been noisy enough if everyone were learning the same thing. But there was only one room and one teacher for all of the children in the different grades. By making the whole school recite aloud, the teacher could be sure that everybody was working.

Abe's hardworking pappy, who had never had any education, didn't think schooling was all that useful out in the wilderness. Time spent in the classroom kept a boy from doing chores. And hadn't he himself gotten along well enough in his own life without ever "larnin' " to read or write or do sums?

Besides all this, Tom Lincoln may not have had too high an opinion of frontier schoolmasters. A teacher in the backwoods was only half-educated himself and had no particular training for his job. And school never lasted more than a few weeks out of the year because the children had to help out at home. These teachers traveled about and could not always be counted on to return when it was time for classes to start again. There were years to come when Abe would be ready for school, but there would be no one around to teach him.

When he was a grown man, Abe added up all the time he had spent in a classroom. Altogether it came to about one year.

A Wilderness Camp

Going to school was not the only way that a curious boy could learn about the world around him. The famous Cumberland Trail was only a stone's throw from the Lincolns' cabin. Abe stood in the doorway and watched families in covered wagons heading out farther west. There were lawyers on horseback going to and from the nearby courthouse. There were peddlers' carts rattling along with their clattering tin pans and pots. Now and then Abe noticed well-dressed people in beautiful carriages.

He also saw white men on horseback selling gangs of black slaves.

Neighbors who were moving away would stop by the Lincoln cabin to say good-bye. Abe listened in silence and tried to understand the conversation. Kentucky was not a good place to stay anymore. Too many slaves were being brought in by the rich people. It made ordinary folks feel even poorer, especially since the slave owners looked down on the hardworking white farmers and called them "trash" or "scrubs."

There were also problems with something called "land titles." Men from the East who had never farmed in Kentucky—or even seen it— were bringing lawsuits against the farmers. Their lawyers would show up in court with "deeds," legal papers that said that others owned the land instead of the families who lived on them. The farmers were called trespassers and squatters. They had to leave the houses they had built and give up their farms.

Even old Daniel Boone—the man who led the first settlers into Kentucky—was cheated out of his property! Over to the northwest in Indiana was "Congress" land that the United

States government was willing to sell for only two dollars an acre if the buyer was willing to clear and farm it. No one could throw you off, and you didn't have to pay for it right away either. What's more, everyone was free and equal in "Indianny" because the law didn't allow anyone to keep a slave there.

Abe's father paid a good deal of attention to talk of Congress land. He had given up his last farm because he couldn't prove to a judge that he owned it. And now someone was trying to take away this farm as well. One day he set off by himself to see what Congress land was like. He was gone for weeks. When he returned, he told his family to start packing. They loaded as much bedding, clothing, and cooking pots as their two animals could carry and set out for their new home.

The beginning of winter was not the best time for a journey. But Tom Lincoln wanted to be settled on his new farm in time for spring planting. During the day, they walked and rode over ice-covered trails. At night they huddled together shivering around a campfire while eating the potatoes and corn dodgers Nancy Lincoln had cooked. Finally they reached their first destination, Thompson's Ferry, on the Kentucky side of the wide Ohio River.

The boatman took them and their belongings across the river to the Indiana shore. Mr. Lincoln rented a covered wagon from the owner of a house near the shore, hitched up his two horses, and climbed aboard with his family.

For a while they traveled more comfortably than before. But the road that took them away from the river soon narrowed into an old Indian trail. No one had ever put an ax to the trees around them. They were huge and grew so close together that the branches above their heads often shut out the sunlight. Thorn bushes and thick brush often blocked the horses' way. Tom Lincoln would have to move on ahead of them to clear the trail. And eight-year-old Abe would get down from the wagon with his own ax to help his father.

Nighttime in that dense dark forest was terrifying even to a boy who was big and strong for his age. Large bears, wolves, and wildcats roamed through the woods. But it was the savage scream of the panthers that filled the pio-

neers with fear. At last Abe's pappy caught sight of the trees he had marked with his ax. The Lincolns were home!

But it was a home without a house. It was the middle of the winter and the Lincoln family needed shelter. The whole family set to work right away. Making poles from trees, they built a shed. They made a roof for it out of bushes and branches. That would have to do for now. There wasn't enough time to put up a real cabin.

This "half-faced camp" on Little Pigeon Creek was open on the side facing south. A fire burned in front of it day and night to keep them warm—and to keep the wild animals away. Here the Lincolns stayed for most of the winter, sleeping on leaves and animal skins they had spread out on the open ground and drinking melted snow. With his Kentucky long rifle and his knife, Abe's pappy hunted for their food, shooting at wild turkey, partridges, rabbits, deer, coon, and even bear. And as soon as he could, he built a log cabin, hanging a bearskin in the doorway to keep out the wind and rain.

There was much to be done in that winter and spring of 1816. The land had to be cleared of trees and underbrush in time for the planting of wheat, corn, and oats. But everyone worked together. And the family relaxed at night when Nancy Lincoln told them Bible stories.

But by the end of the next winter, Mrs. Lincoln grew too weak to take care of her family. She had come down with the "milk sick."

No one knew for certain what caused the dreaded disease. Some thought it came from drinking the milk of a cow that had eaten the leaves of a plant called white snake root. There was no cure. The children could do nothing but stand by their mother's bedside, watching her waste away. Nancy died and the whole family was very sad. When Tom Lincoln worked as a carpenter back in Kentucky, he sometimes built coffins for other people. Now he made one for his own wife. Nine-year-old Abe whittled the pegs that nailed it together.

Nothing was the same after that. Sarah, who was only eleven, tried her best to take her mother's place at washing, mending, and cooking. But these tasks were too much for her. For months at a time Tom Lincoln barely said a word to anyone. He stopped taking care of himself or his children. The cabin grew filthy. So did Abe and Sarah. Soon their clothes turned to rags.

Meanwhile, Tom Lincoln had an idea. He waited until fall when the crops were harvested before telling his children that he had to go away. Abe's cousin Dennis Hanks had been living with them since his own parents died of the milk sick in the same outbreak of that disease that had taken his mother, Nancy. Tom Lincoln asked seventeen-year-old Dennis to watch over the children. Then he took his rifle down from its pegs over the fireplace and left the cabin. The three youngsters watched him disappear on foot into the woods without knowing where he was going or when he would be back.

Days turned into weeks while the three of them waited for Tom Lincoln's return. While Dennis hunted for meat to put on the table, Abe and Sarah tried to get along as best they could. But the empty feeling of being without either a mother or a father grew in them. They became even dirtier and more forlorn.

Then one afternoon in December they saw a four-horse covered wagon come into the clearing. Putting down the reins, Tom Lincoln jumped off, saying, "Here's your new mammy."

While Abe, Sarah, and Dennis gaped, a large woman with a kind, rosy face got down after their pappy, followed by her own three children, John, Matilda, and another little girl named Sarah.

Abe's New Mother

Sarah Bush Johnson and Tom Lincoln had been friends since childhood. When Tom Lincoln heard the news that Sarah's husband was dead, he started thinking about her as a possible new mother for his children. As soon as he could leave the farm, he walked a hundred miles back to Kentucky.

"Mrs. Johnson," he said, "I have no wife and you have no husband. I came a-purpose to marry you. I knowed you from a gal and you knowed me from a boy. I've no time to lose; and if you're willing, let it be done straight off."

21

Sarah Johnson had always thought well of Tom Lincoln. He was one of the few men on the frontier who didn't drink hard liquor or curse. And she felt that her children needed a father. Wasting no time, she married him, sold her house, and packed her finest belongings and her own three children into a wagon.

Abe's pappy must have been happy and embarrassed at the same time. The youngsters standing so shyly in front of the new Mrs. Lincoln were filthy. But she opened her heart to them at once and took them into her arms as if they were her own. Like her own children, they were soon well-scrubbed, well-fed, and wearing clean clothes.

Over the next few weeks Abe, his sister, and their cousin Dennis watched their little house become a real home. Out of the wagon had come a beautiful black walnut chest of drawers, a feather mattress, a nice table, and shiny pots and pans. But the new mammy didn't stop there. She turned her attention to the cabin itself, which had never been properly finished.

It wasn't very long before Tom Lincoln had

covered the dirt floor with a proper wooden one. The door soon opened on real hinges made of leather. Since glass was hard to find out west, he covered the window with oiled paper. And then Tom made his large family some fine beds and chairs. He also got around to filling in the spaces between the logs in the roof so that rain and snow stopped coming into the loft where Abe and Dennis slept. With Sarah Bush Lincoln at the center of things (there were three Sarahs under one roof now!), the little cabin became tidy, cozy, and full of good cheer.

But Mrs. Lincoln cared about much more than the way her home and her children looked. She saw that, of all the children in the house, Abe had the most curiosity and the greatest desire to learn. She encouraged him and showed that she believed in him. And that gave him enough confidence in himself to last him all his life, even when he became a famous politician. "All that I am or hope to be," he once said when he was grown up, "I owe to my angel mother."

One of Abe's first ambitions was to go back

to school. The years were passing swiftly, and he hadn't been in a classroom since leaving Kentucky. His angel mother had to work hard to convince her husband to let eleven-year-old Abe put down his ax and his hoe and go off again to blab school.

Abe was used to all kinds of weather. He didn't mind the four-and-a-half-mile walk to and from school. It gave him the time to think about the new words he had learned or to take a pointed stick and practice writing in the dirt. At night he would pull a piece of charcoal from the fireplace and write on the back of the coal shovel. But when Abe marked up the wood floor, his father threw him out of the house and wouldn't let him come back in for hours.

It was Dennis who finally solved Abe's problem. He whittled pens out of turkey buzzard quills and made ink from blackberry briarroot. Then he found some wrapping paper for Abe to practice on. One day Abe made himself a scrapbook from a few sheets of real writing paper that he managed to get hold of. On one of them he wrote:

Abraham Lincoln
his hand and pen
he will be good
but God knows When.

Abe enjoyed practicing his handwriting and spelling, but reading was his greatest joy. Finding books to read was a big problem, however. Back east there were bookstores and free public libraries. Benjamin Franklin, the great publisher and inventor, had started the first public library in Philadelphia. But Abe lived on the frontier. The only book in the Lincoln house, as in so many other poor folks' homes, was the family Bible. It wasn't long before Abe had memorized many parts of it, but that wasn't enough for him.

"My best friend," Dennis once heard him say, "would be the man who could get me a book."

Making up his mind to be that friend, Dennis cut firewood for neighbors to earn the money to buy Abe a book. Nobody knows for certain which book Dennis bought. But when Abe finished reading it, he walked long distances to borrow others.

One book Abe read was *Aesop's Fables*. He also read *Robinson Crusoe*, a novel about a man who is shipwrecked on a deserted island. Since Abe spent so much time on his own in the woods, he could understand Crusoe, who had only his own two hands and brain to help him survive.

But Abe's favorite hero was the man who led the American Revolution and who became the country's first president. The most famous book about George Washington in those days was a biography by Parson Weems. From it, Abe learned a good deal about the decency and honesty of the man who was the Father of our Country. That also started him thinking about the sacrifices that great people like Washington—and hardworking ones like his own grandfather—had made to create the United States of America.

"I remember," Abe said after he became President, "all the accounts there given of the battlefields and struggles for the liberties of the country. . . . I recollect thinking then, boy even though I was, that there must have been something more than common that these men struggled for."

The more Abe read, the more he wanted to read. But in the daytime his chores kept him busy. And at night there were six youngsters and two adults crowded into the single room where the family lived. Candles were scarce, so the fireplace was the cabin's only source of light. During the cold weather everyone wanted to sit close to the burning logs. Yet somehow Abe found time and room to spread out on the floor in front of the fire and read aloud to himself softly the way he had learned at blab school.

His mother wouldn't allow anyone in the house to tease Abe. "Abe is going to be a great man someday," she would say about her adopted son, "and I won't have anybody hindering him!"

Rail Splitting and Flatboating

Tom Lincoln wanted to train his son in carpentry and was disappointed when Abe showed so little interest. But he could still put the boy to work earning money. At seventeen Abe was already close to six feet four inches tall. He weighed about two hundred pounds. When he swung his ax, he buried it deeper into a tree than most people had ever seen before.

Abe's father decided to hire out his son to some new settlers who needed a lad to clear their fields and split the fallen logs into rails for fences. It was the law then that until a child

turned twenty-one his father could keep all of his earnings. The family could use every penny of the sixteen cents a day that Abe would be paid.

Soon Abe was hired out to do all sorts of odd jobs, everything from minding babies to plowing fields. He got the work done, and he was good-humored about it. But people didn't quite know what to make of him. Every chance he got he would pull a book out of his pocket and start to read.

It was easy for anyone who hired Abe to see that here was a young man who would rather turn a page than split a log. When a farmer told him one day that he was lazy, Abe laughed and said, "My father taught me to work; but he never taught me to love it."

One of the things that he *did* love was going to the general store in the tiny village of Gentryville. People from the backwoods went there to shop and talk. They would sit around the wood stove or the cracker barrel listening while someone read to them from the newspaper that had come all the way from Louisville, Kentucky.

The news gave people issues to think about.

Was it right or wrong to let slaves who had escaped from their masters be recaptured in the free Northern states and sent back South? Where should the money come from to build roads in the West?

Abe would read aloud from the speeches that Kentucky senator Henry Clay had made in Washington. Topics included putting an end to slavery in the nation's capital and having the federal government improve the roads and waterways in the West. Abe loved Clay's speeches and wished he could make some of his own.

Abe also told funny stories. He had such a good imagination and sense of humor that people would gather round him just to hear him spin his yarns.

Mr. Gentry, the storekeeper, decided to offer him a job behind the counter. It wasn't just because Abe could read and write, add and subtract. He was well aware of the fact that whenever Abe was around, customers would stay and listen to his stories. The longer they stayed, Mr. Gentry found out, the more time he had to interest them in buying things.

Abe enjoyed his new job. It was much more

relaxing than pushing a plow or swinging an ax. But it wasn't helping him to find his place in the world.

After having an experience in court, Abe decided he might one day want to become a lawyer. One day he was down by the Ohio River at a place called Bates Landing. Abe had just built a little boat, hoping to use it to make extra money running errands for people. He was delighted when two men had him row them and their trunks out to a steamboat in the middle of the river. Abe was speechless when each of them tossed him a silver half-dollar. Never before in his life had he earned that much money for less than a day's work.

But suddenly he was in trouble. The operators of a ferry that ran between the two shores arrested him and took him to court on the Kentucky side. They claimed that the law did not allow anybody but them to charge money to ferry passengers across that part of the river.

When it was Abe's turn to defend himself, he made a little speech. "Judge," he said, "*across* the river doesn't mean the same thing as only going to the *middle* of it. That's like saying that having a mouthful of pork is the same thing as eating the whole hog."

Squire Pate, who was the justice of the peace, ruled in Abe's favor. But he did more than that. He lent this convincing young man a law book and invited him to watch other cases being tried.

In spite of the squire's friendship and Abe's talent for winning an argument, there didn't seem to be any chance that anyone as poor and uneducated as Abe would ever become a lawyer. But there was much adventure to be had on the river. In pioneer days when there were few roads, rivers were the main highways. Any man who worked on a passenger boat or a flatboat carrying cargo traveled great distances and saw new sights.

It was a dream come true when the storekeeper asked Abe to help his son, Allan, take a cargo of grain, whiskey, and live pigs all the way down to the great city of New Orleans. It was going to be a journey of a thousand miles!

Together with Allan Gentry, Abe built a flatboat. It wasn't entirely flat, though. They had to put up sides high enough to keep the animals from falling off. And they had to protect themselves from Indian arrows and attacks by river pirates. When it was finished, the boat had neither sails nor a motor, only a big oar to steer it while floating downstream. Pushing off from the Indiana shore, they headed out into the center of the river. Strong currents carried them south to the junction of the Ohio River and the mighty Mississippi.

Everything went peacefully on the Mississippi until they tied up their boat on shore one night to get some sleep. By the time a noise awakened them, a gang of robbers were already coming aboard. Abe and Allan grabbed wooden clubs and fought them off. Since there was no way of knowing whether the river pirates might return with more men, Abe and Allan thought it would be safer to pull away from the shore. They did not touch land again until they arrived in New Orleans.

The great city with its cobblestone streets, fine houses, and people speaking many languages was fascinating for the young men. But in a different way, so was the slave market. The two had been traveling in slave territory ever since their boat had floated into the Mississippi. But they hadn't seen what keeping human beings in bondage was like until then.

They stared at men, women, and children being touched, handled, and sold at auction like horses and cattle. They watched groups of slaves in chains and handcuffs being marched through the streets on their way to the big cotton plantations of the South.

Abe came from a family that did not think slavery was right or fair. He could not even bear to see a small animal cruelly treated. But whatever he thought about that trip, he kept it to himself. He and Allan sold the cargo and the raft. Then they bought sugar, tobacco, and cotton for Allan's father's store and boarded a steamboat to carry them home.

When Abe returned to Indiana, he learned that his family was about to move again. The farm wasn't doing well, and all around them the milk sick was once more beginning to strike. Tom Lincoln had decided to join four other families heading for Illinois. He had heard that the flatter ground there was better for growing crops.

Abe had hoped to start living on his own when he turned twenty-one in a couple of months. But he couldn't let his family down. All winter he helped his father build an ox wagon. Huge trees had to be cut down and sawed across to make the wooden wheels. Logs had to be split into floorboards and pegs whittled out to use as nails. Three days after Abe's birthday the wagon was finished and loaded with the family's possessions.

Abe knew that he would have to go along to help his family get settled. But he wanted to have some money of his own when he got there. Before setting out, Abe went to the store in Gentryville and bought the dry goods he would need to be a peddler. For two weeks Abe drove the oxen. On the way he stopped at every wilderness farm they passed and sold his wares.

John Hanks, a friend of the family who had gone on ahead to Illinois, picked out a piece of land for them. It wasn't on the open prairie that Tom Lincoln had heard was good for growing corn. Hanks knew that the Lincolns could never be happy without trees on their land. He found a place for them on a little wooded hill overlooking the Sangamon River.

But the next winter Tom Lincoln decided that, trees or not, this place had been a mistake. So the Lincolns moved on once again, this time to flat land in Illinois called Goose Neck Prairie. Abe helped his father build yet another cabin. Abe teamed up with John Hanks, and together they hired themselves out to neighbors as rail splitters. John would chop the trees down, then Abe would split them into rails.

Abe did everything he could to stay cheerful, but he knew that rail splitting wasn't getting him anywhere closer to his dream of becoming a lawyer. One day John Hanks told Abe about a storekeeper up north on the Sangamon River who wanted rivermen to take a flatboat to New Orleans.

It was Abe's second trip to the city that was the center of the slave trade. When Abe returned, he couldn't keep silent.

"In May we landed in New Orleans," he told a relative. "There it was we saw Negroes chained, maltreated, whipped, and scourged. If I ever get a chance to hit slavery," he said, "I'll hit it hard."

That was brave talk for a poor, half-educated young man from the wilderness. Abe knew of one small step that he could take to improve his situation. The man who had hired him to go down to New Orleans had also offered him a job as a storekeeper in New Salem, a small village on the Sangamon River in Illinois. Making a bundle of his few belongings, Abe tied it to a stick, which he slung over his shoulder. After saying good-bye to his family, he set off for New Salem on foot.

New Salem

It was a summer's day when Abe arrived in New Salem. He noticed a line of people standing in front of a table. Growing curious, he strolled over and learned that they were waiting their turn to vote in an election. One by one each man (women did not have the right to vote in those days) called out his name and whom he was voting for.

The person behind the desk was hot and tired. Some say that he noticed Abe and asked the young man hopefully, "Can you write?"

"Reckon I can make a few rabbit tracks," Abe answered.

"Then please sit down and help me."

That was how Abe met Mentor Graham, the town's schoolmaster. Graham spent the day listening to Abe exchanging ideas with people. He thought that Abe made good sense when he talked about the need for the government in Washington to help improve the roads and waterways out west.

Abe was speaking from his own experience. He knew that the rivers had to be deepened where they were too shallow. Abe's second flatboating trip had started in New Salem. The Sangamon River was low at that time of the year, and his boat had gotten stuck on top of the mill dam. The pigs on board squealed in terror.

A crowd had gathered by the shore to watch. Abe called for someone to row a boat out to him, and he unloaded the pigs into it. He bored a hole in the front of the boat so that water would rush in and tip it forward. Then he rolled some pork barrels from the back to the front. Finally the boat slid over the dam.

After that came the task of plugging the hole, bailing out the water, and getting all the pigs back on board.

Mentor Graham also saw that Abe had the ability to get people to listen when he spoke. But the *way* that young Lincoln presented his ideas made him seem more ignorant than he really was.

"Abe," Graham told him, "don't say 'if *them* bends in the Sangamon River was straightened out.' It's *those* bends, and the verb is plural."

Abe borrowed a book of grammar and studied it every free minute he could find. In the evenings, after leaving the store where he worked, he'd go to Mentor Graham's house to get more help with his English. The schoolmaster, who also taught him mathematics and geometry, was proud of his oldest pupil. One day he invited Abe to come to a meeting of a debating club, where people discussed every topic from taxes to better roads to slavery.

At this point the two main political parties in the country were the Democratic and the Whig. The Democratic party did not want to see the states lose any power to the federal government. And the Whig party believed that the government in Washington should do more to help develop different parts of the country. The Whig party was also less friendly to slavery than the Democratic party. The Whigs did not want to see slavery spread into any of the new states that were being admitted to the Union.

Mentor Graham, along with most of the members of his debating club, belonged to the Whigs. They agreed with the schoolmaster that Abe's speeches were very convincing. They thought he should enter politics and get elected to the state legislature.

This young man who came out of the wilderness was able to speak about important issues without sounding stuck-up. And people were constantly saying that Abe was one store clerk who'd never cheat a customer. Everyone in town heard about the time Abe accidentally overcharged an old woman at the store for some dry goods. When he realized his mistake, he walked miles to her farm to give her back the six cents.

But honesty wasn't Abe's only claim to fame in the frontier town of New Salem. Folks also knew how Abe Lincoln had licked Jack Armstrong, the town bully, in a wrestling match in front of the store. Bets had been taken on the fight—and Armstrong's gang of young toughs, called the Clary Grove Boys, didn't like what had happened to their champion. They closed in on Abe. But Armstrong broke it up. He said he had been beaten in a fair fight.

Before Abe could run for the legislature, however, he had to follow the custom of sending an announcement letter to the newspapers. In the letter he was expected to tell the voters what sort of person he was.

Taking a long walk in the woods, he reminded himself how George Washington had once answered that very same question. The Father of our Country had wanted to live his life in such a way that he would earn the high opinion of his fellow men. Abraham Lincoln wrote the same thing in his announcement letter.

Abe's campaign was interrupted by an Indian War. Years before, Black Hawk, chief of the Sacs, had let himself be tricked into selling tribal land in northwestern Illinois. But the white men had broken their promise to Black Hawk. The Sacs were not allowed to hunt, fish, or plant corn on this land, though they were supposed to have this right. Now the tribe was close to starvation. With five hundred painted warriors, Black Hawk crossed over to Illinois from Wisconsin to drive the settlers out.

Abe did not live at a time when white people thought about how unfairly Native Americans were treated. His grandfather had been killed by Indians, and many settlers still faced the same danger. When the governor called for volunteers to help the United States Army drive the Sacs out of Illinois, Abe mounted his horse and joined up.

The young men from New Salem, including the Clary Grove Boys, picked Abe to be their captain. This was the first election he ever won. It was also the one that gave him the most satisfaction. The man he defeated was a mill owner who had once cheated him out of a day's pay.

For three months Abe rode with his men. They galloped through deep mud, slept on the ground in the cold rain, and buried scalped settlers. But they never came up against the forces of Black Hawk. The chief was too clever and quick for his enemies. Again and again he and his outnumbered warriors escaped the traps that were set for them.

During this time, Abe saw only one Indian. Like Black Hawk, he was a very old man. But unlike Black Hawk, he was no warrior. The Indian came into Abe's camp carrying a letter from an army general. The letter said that the Indian should be left alone because he hadn't taken part in the fighting. But Lincoln's men wanted to shoot this Indian.

Abe ordered them to stop, but his men refused to obey him. So Abe stood between his men and the intended victim. "Lincoln," someone cried when they saw he was ready to fight, "you're bigger and heavier than we are."

Abe lowered his hands. "You can guard against that. Choose your weapons."

Abe had never fought a duel in his life, but he meant what he said. When his men saw that he was ready to die to save the Indian, they backed off.

The only way that the heavily outnumbered

Sacs could keep from being beaten was to set traps and ambushes, strike their enemies suddenly, and vanish instantly. But they could not go on forever. The Illinois volunteers and the army, together with a hundred Indian allies, drove the Sacs back into Wisconsin. Black Hawk was finally captured, and his exhausted braves surrendered.

The war was over, and everyone could go home. But someone had stolen Abe's horse. He had to hitch rides or walk much of the four hundred miles back to New Salem.

Jack of All Trades

By the time he got back, Abe was left with very little time to meet people and make speeches before election day. That didn't matter in New Salem, where he was already well known. But people who lived in other parts of Sangamon County had never heard of him, so Abe lost the election.

He was disappointed but not downhearted. Almost everyone who *did* know Abe had voted to send him to the state legislature as their representative. In the next two years he would have the opportunity to meet new people. Then he could try running for office again.

Meanwhile, he was a poor man. He still wasn't the lawyer he longed to be. Yet he had to earn a living. Abe bought a store for a very low price with the help of a partner and some borrowed money.

Unfortunately, times were hard and customers had very little money to spend. Abe's partner wasn't very helpful either. He had such a bad drinking problem that he couldn't be relied on to tend the store. But then, neither could Abe, whose thoughts were on other things. He was often so absentminded that he didn't pay attention to the customers. They decided to shop elsewhere. The store lost money, and soon Abe found himself deeply in debt.

One day a covered wagon pulled up in front of his store, and a man came in wanting to sell a barrel. The barrel was old and broken and filled with things that Abe couldn't use. But it was easy to see that the man was very poor and that his family was hungry. Abe fed the family and bought the barrel.

It was weeks before he bothered to look

inside the barrel. To his amazement, he found a copy of *Blackstone's Commentaries,* the book one had to study to become a lawyer. With so few customers coming into the shop, Abe had plenty of time to study his new book.

While he was teaching himself about the law, Abe was offered the chance to become the assistant to the county surveyor. His job would be to map out and measure off plots of land for the new settlers in that part of Illinois. Ordinarily it would take six months to learn everything a surveyor needed to know. Abe put aside his copy of *Blackstone's Commentaries* and threw himself into his new studies. Night after night he worked hard and often went to his store the next day without having gotten much sleep. In six weeks he was ready to go to work.

Meanwhile, Abe was appointed New Salem's postmaster and turned part of his shop into a post office. To save people the trouble of coming into town for their mail, Abe tucked their letters under his hat and delivered them when he rode off to do his surveying.

People thought it was "right neighborly" of him to drop off their mail along the way. Often

they would ask Abe to come "sit a spell" over a glass of milk. If some farmer had a problem with the deed to his land, Abe would pull out a lawbook and give the farmer advice. Abe never charged any money for giving this help. He hadn't forgotten all the people who had been thrown off their land back in Kentucky. Besides, Abe wasn't allowed to take money. He didn't have a license to be a lawyer yet. He still had to pass the bar examination.

But what he *could* do in the meantime was become a Whig candidate for the next election to the Illinois House of Representatives. By this time Abe had gained enough popularity to win the election.

There was just one problem. Although Abe earned money from surveying, almost all of it went to pay off his debts. He didn't have the fare for the stagecoach to Vandalia, the state capital. And when he got there, he'd look mighty peculiar wearing a pair of linen pants that ended six inches above his feet, and were held up only by a half-broken suspender.

A kindly person lent Abe the money he needed to buy a "stovepipe" hat, a new pair of shoes, and a suit that fit. And when he finally climbed into the stagecoach, he was cheered by his many proud friends.

Abe was very lucky to have a friend named John T. Stuart, who was already serving his second term in the legislature. To save on rent money, Abe moved in with him. Since Stuart was the leader of the Whigs, their home became a meeting place for party members.

Abe learned a lot by listening. The representatives and senators didn't wait for the voting to take place on a bill. They got together beforehand and traded votes.

"Listen here," one man might say. "Folks in my county want a new bridge. Folks in yours want that road fixed. I'll vote for your bill if you'll vote for mine."

Abe saw how deals were made, but he never voted for a bill he thought was wrong. Soon he became John Stuart's assistant in the legislature. When Abe ran for reelection the next summer, he got an even larger vote than before.

This was a time when great sadness came into Abe's life. He had been very close to Ann Rutledge, daughter of the president of his debating society in New Salem. When Ann came down with a disease the settlers called "bilious fever," he rushed to her side and caught it from her.

Because Abe was very strong, he soon recovered. But there was nothing that could be done to save his beloved Ann. He took it very hard when she died. There are some who say that he couldn't eat or sleep. For days at a time he wandered through the woods, half-crazed with grief.

When Abe returned to the state capital, he threw himself into his work. His friend John Stuart had left the legislature to run for the United States Congress, and Abe became leader of the Whigs.

At last Abe passed the bar examination and became a lawyer! He and John Stuart became partners and opened a law practice in Springfield. Then the state capital was moved to Springfield. Abe moved there from New Salem. Their little law office was above the county courtroom—and by opening a trapdoor in the floor Abe could hear the cases being tried.

It wasn't long before people realized that

"lawyer Lincoln" was good at solving problems. He tried his best to satisfy both sides without going to court. But when he did have to argue a case, he usually won. More likely than not, it was after he made the judge and jury burst out laughing.

But Abe was dead serious when it came to the slavery issue. One day he read about a newspaper editor in a slave state who had written articles protesting slavery. Mobs had chased him out of one town after another, set his office on fire, and shot him to death. Abe gave a speech at a discussion club about the right of every person to say what he or she believed in—and to be protected by the law. His speech was printed in the *Sangamon Journal*. After that, whenever he spoke publicly, large crowds showed up to hear him.

Election to Congress

A be finally met someone who helped him get over his loneliness. Her name was Mary Todd. She was very bright, merry, and witty. But she came from a wealthy Kentucky family that had always looked down on humble folks like the Lincolns. Besides, she was being courted by a young Democratic politician named Stephen Douglas. He was rich and he had fine manners. Mary was very ambitious. Young Douglas was already an important man, while Abe was just becoming well known. When asked which of the two men she intended to marry, Mary said, "The one who has the best chance of being president."

She meant Abe, not Douglas. She saw the true greatness inside of him that others had yet to discover. And she also loved him for his goodness. But Mary also had her problems with Abe. He was often too sad to be good company. Sometimes he was so absentminded or busy that he forgot all about her.

Abe loved Mary very dearly. But he didn't like it when she grew cross with him just because he couldn't stop working to take her to parties and concerts. They quarreled a lot and broke up more than once. After two years they decided that it was hard to be together, but it was impossible to be apart. They got married on November 4, 1842.

The new Mrs. Lincoln may have had a sharp temper, but she also had great faith in her husband. She didn't mind that they had to move into a room above a tavern. A year later Robert, their first child, was born. Abe's law practice was growing all the time and it wasn't long before he bought a pleasant house for his family to live in.

There were many nights, however, when

Abe didn't have a chance to sleep in his new house. The judge who held court in Springfield also heard cases in seven other counties on his "circuit." Lawyers who followed him from courtroom to courtroom were said to be "riding the circuit." In all kinds of weather Abe would climb up on a horse or into a buggy and drive off across the open prairie. It was very tiring. But by traveling around the state, Abe met many new people, and everywhere he went he made friends.

Abe never allowed his thoughts to stray very far from politics. In 1846 he felt he was ready to run for the United States Congress. His Whig supporters gave him $200 to spend on his campaign. After Abe won the election to the House of Representatives, he returned what was left over: $199.25.

"All the traveling I did was on my own horse," Abe explained. "Wherever I went my friends entertained me. And I only had to spend seventy-five cents one day for a barrel of cider to treat some farmhands."

Abe's honesty was appreciated then, but it got him into trouble very soon after he arrived

in Washington. Fighting had broken out between the United States and Mexico over the land that would soon become Texas and New Mexico. Each side blamed the other for causing the war. Abe was certain that the United States had started it, and he said so in Congress.

Many people in Washington called him a traitor. And even back in Illinois some of his closest friends turned against him.

Abe was heartbroken. "My future is behind me," he said, thinking he would never win another election.

But Congressman Lincoln had something more important on his mind than his political career. From the windows of the Capitol Building, Abe could see a slave market. Walking down Pennsylvania Avenue, he watched rows of black people being led around in chains.

One day in Congress Abe stood up and asked for a law to put an end to slavery in the nation's capital. He wanted to pay slave owners for losing their "property." The bill was not passed. At the end of his term Abe went home to Springfield to practice law, play with his children, and live the life of an ordinary man.

A House Divided

Over the next few years Abe "rode the circuit" again. Though he worked very hard, he didn't make a lot of money. He charged his clients much smaller fees than the other lawyers did. And if someone who was very poor came to him for help, he would take on the case for nothing. When he felt sorry for his clients, he even *gave* them money.

Abe's greatest concern, however, was national politics. Stephen Douglas, who had once been his rival for Mary Todd's hand in marriage, was now a United States senator. Douglas had talked Congress into putting an end to the famous Missouri Compromise. The compromise had drawn a line across the United States from the east coast to the west coast. Any new state coming into the Union which was south of that line was allowed to have slavery. But in any new state north of that line, slavery was forbidden. This agreement was supposed to keep peace between the Southern states and the Northern states.

But Douglas's new bill would change all that by allowing the voters in the huge western territories of Kansas and Nebraska to decide for themselves whether or not slavery should exist in their states.

Abe knew that this new bill would seem very fair to some people. But did anyone have the right to vote on whether someone else should be free or in chains? Besides, who would these "voters" be? Only white men had the right to vote.

Both slave owners and abolitionists—people who wanted to end slavery—were rushing people into Kansas to increase the number of voters who agreed with them. Both sides were armed and angry. There were shootings. Houses and farms were burned to the ground. The territory was quickly becoming known as Bleeding Kansas.

Lincoln could hardly think about his law practice anymore. Now was the time to keep the promise he had once made to himself to "hit slavery hard." He traveled throughout Illinois making speeches. The Whig party he had belonged to no longer existed—it had fallen apart over the issue of slavery. He joined the Republican party, which had been formed in 1854 to combat the spread of slavery. The members of the new Republican party included some former Whigs and some Democrats who were antislavery.

In 1858 Lincoln became the Republican candidate to run against Douglas for senator. Lincoln told the men who nominated him that slavery had to be stopped from spreading. If it could be held back, it would eventually die out altogether. America could not forever remain half slave and half free. It was as if America were one big house. In some rooms there were many people chained to the walls, but in other rooms all people could live as if God had truly created them equal. How long could freedom be kept in the front parlor while there was slavery going on in the kitchen?

"A house divided against itself cannot stand," Abe said. When he challenged Stephen Douglas to meet him in debate, Douglas did not like the idea. He was much better known than Lincoln, and these debates would give his opponent a chance to become famous, too. But he had to accept, or he would appear to be afraid of Lincoln.

The two men agreed to hold seven debates throughout the state.

Everywhere they went, great parades, banners, and marching bands greeted them. Senator Douglas would arrive in a splendid carriage pulled by six white horses. Abe would pull up in a hay wagon. When the two men climbed to the speakers' platform, the man now called "Old Abe" stood almost a foot and a half taller than Douglas, the "Little Giant."

Douglas defended the right of the white people of Kansas to choose whether their state should be slave or free. Abe did not agree that

white people had the right to decide that black people should be slaves. That, said Abe, would be like telling someone, "*You* toil and work and earn bread—and *I'll* eat it."

Douglas was shaken when most people in the crowds supported Abe. Reporters from all over the country wrote articles about the debates. The whole nation learned what Abe had to say about the dangers of letting slavery spread into the new territories of the Northwest. In the North there were many who agreed with him.

At election time Abe got the most votes. But that didn't mean he had been elected senator. In those days people didn't vote directly for their candidate. They cast their ballots to tell their representatives in the state legislature whom *they* should vote for. Douglas had more power in the Illinois state legislature than Abe did, and when all the votes were counted, Lincoln had lost the election. He said he felt like a boy who had stubbed his toe. "It hurt too much to laugh, and he was too big to cry." But later he said, "A slip is not a fall!"

Yet in spite of this loss, some newspapers in

Illinois and other nearby states were calling for Abe to be nominated by the Republican party for the upcoming presidential election. And when the delegates to the Republican party met in May 1860 to nominate their candidate, they *did* choose him.

Lincoln's nomination angered and worried those people who were for slavery. There were warnings that the Southern states would "secede"—or break away—from the United States of America and set up a country of their own if Abe was to be elected president.

Abe tried his best to calm their fears. Even though he thought slavery was wrong, he would never force the states that already had it to give it up. He said he simply wanted to stop the expansion of slavery. Abe believed, however, that slavery would die out over a period of time if it could be kept from spreading.

But the proslavery leaders did not believe that Abe meant to keep his word. The Democratic party split in half. The secessionists nominated a man named John C. Breckinridge to run against Abe. Those Democrats who wanted the South to stay in the Union, no matter who won the election, chose the Little Giant, Stephen Douglas, as their candidate.

The Democratic votes were split between Abe's two opponents, while Abe got all the Republican ones. On November 6, 1860, he was elected the sixteenth President of the United States of America.

President Abraham Lincoln

Abe boarded a train for Washington several days before his inauguration because he wanted to make special stops in other cities. He was on his way to deliver a speech in Harrisburg, Pennsylvania, when the great detective Allan Pinkerton warned him about a murder plot. The attack was going to take place in Baltimore, Maryland, where a secret society had been formed to kill Lincoln before he could become president.

Baltimore was filled with white people who hated Lincoln enough to kill him. It was also the best place for an assassination attempt to succeed. At that time no train locomotive could go all the way through the city. Lincoln's train would have to stop at the station at one end of town for the engine to be uncoupled and replaced by horses. Then the horses would pull the rest of the train to the far side of town, where another locomotive would be attached to it for the last stage of the journey. At that point the train would head for Washington. But the assassins had promised themselves that Lincoln would never leave the city alive. They planned to attack the President's car while the slow-moving horses were pulling it.

That evening Abe made his speech as planned. But afterward, he put on a different hat than the tall silk one he was famous for wearing and quietly slipped into a waiting carriage. Abe was whisked through the night to the Harrisburg railroad station and secretly put on board another train. It was like a ghost train, with only one car and no lights.

Abe's secret train traveled through the darkness to Philadelphia. There, he was smuggled aboard a third train. It was filled with passengers bound for Washington. No one except a woman detective working for Pinkerton knew that Abe was on board. She had reserved a sleeping berth for her "invalid brother." Abe climbed into the berth, pulled the curtains shut, and stayed hidden until the train arrived safely in Washington.

On Inauguration Day, March 4, 1861, Abe stood out in the open on a platform to take the oath of office. Worried policemen sat among the onlookers, watching for the slightest sign that someone might pull a gun.

Abe was worried, too—about the survival of the United States of America. Months earlier, in December 1860, South Carolina had seceded from the Union. By February 8, 1861, the Southern states had set up the Confederate States of America with Jefferson Davis as president. The whole world was waiting to learn whether as President he would allow the Southern states to secede without a fight.

Abe was the last man on earth who wanted to see Americans killing one another in a civil war. In his speech he assured the Southern states that he would not force them to give up slavery if they would stay in the Union. But the oath he was about to take required him to do everything in his power to keep, preserve, protect, and defend the Union. Lincoln was very loyal to the Constitution. He believed that all the states had agreed to it and therefore they must all uphold it. Abraham Lincoln placed his left hand on the Bible, raised his right hand, and took the oath of office.

In the North and the South everyone was waiting to see what would happen next. And soon all eyes were turned upon an island in the harbor of Charleston, South Carolina.

Fort Sumter stood on that tiny piece of land in South Carolina, the first state to have seceded from the Union. It still flew the flag of the United States. Confederate troops rolled their cannons up to the shore, aimed them at the fort, and quietly waited to see what President Lincoln would do.

Instead of surrendering Fort Sumter to the Confederate troops, Abe sent ships with food for the American soldiers on the island. On April 12, 1861, Confederate shells bombarded the walls of the fort. The terrible Civil War, which was to last four long years, had begun.

The South had fewer men to train as soldiers, fewer factories to make weapons, and less money to buy what it needed to fight the war. But one of its generals, Robert E. Lee, was a much better leader than any of the Union generals. For the first year and a half of the war, Lee's army won battle after battle. There were times when it looked as if Washington itself might be captured.

Abe suffered deeply because of all the young people on both sides who were being killed. There were times when the only happiness he got was from his children. The oldest boy, Robert, was away at school. But young Willie and Tad were allowed to run freely around the White House. When they barged into an important meeting, Abe didn't become angry. He only smiled at them and listened to what they had to say.

The war became part of the children's games. They had a doll named Jack that they kept dressed like a soldier. One day they pretended to find him asleep on guard duty. In the real army the punishment for this crime was death. So they went outside and began to dig Jack's grave. When the gardener found out why they were making a hole in the rose garden, he said, "Why don't you ask your father to pardon him?"

Willie and Tad rushed into their father's office with Jack and pleaded for the doll's life. Turning round in his chair, their father wrote on a piece of paper, "The doll Jack is pardoned by order of the President. A. Lincoln."

When he heard his sons run off down the hall, he sighed and said to his secretary, "I wish all pardons were that easy."

Whenever he could, Abe took pity on soldiers who were condemned to be shot. He knew that as commander-in-chief of his country he was supposed to be firm. But when a tearful mother would come to plead for the life of her young son, his heart would go out to her. If Abe could find some good reason to save her boy, he would send out an order that said, "I guess we'll have to let him off this time" or "I don't believe shooting this man will do him any good."

But not even the President of the United

States could save anyone from illness. His son Willie came down with a high fever from which he never recovered. When the boy died, Abe's sadness was very deep. But for Mrs. Lincoln it was much worse. Her grief was so terrible that there were many who thought she had lost her mind.

The Emancipation Proclamation

Abe was receiving letters all the time pleading with him to put an end to slavery right away. A book written by Harriet Beecher Stowe, called *Uncle Tom's Cabin,* had helped millions of Americans to realize that slavery was cruel and inhuman. But what could he do? Most of the slaves were in the rebellious South, where Union Armies had met one defeat after another.

Abe had kept border states like Kentucky loyal to the Union by allowing them to continue the practice of slavery. He offered to have the government buy the freedom of the slaves in these states, but he was refused. At this time there was nothing more Abe could do for slaves in the North. However, the Southern states had not stayed loyal, so Abe was not bound by any promise to them.

He began to work on an emancipation proclamation that would free slaves in the Confederate states. When it was finished, he read it to his cabinet. Secretary of State William H. Seward begged Abe not to sign it while the Union was still losing the war. That would just make the President look weak and desperate. Seward told Abe to wait "until you can give it to the country supported by military success." Abe agreed, but where was the success he needed?

General Lee's troops crossed over the Potomac River into Northern territory. On September 17, 1862, there was a battle at Antietam in Maryland. When Lee saw that he couldn't win it, he pulled his men back across the river. This was hardly the big victory Abe had hoped for. His own general, George B. McClellan, seemed too afraid of Lee to chase after him. Still, it was enough of a triumph for the President to issue the Emancipation Proclamation on September 22, 1862.

It provided that starting January 1, 1863, all persons held as slaves in any of the states that were "in rebellion" would be "forever free."

The proclamation by itself didn't actually put an end to slavery anywhere. It didn't apply at all to the black people in the states that had stayed in the Union. (Although Abe was sure they would be freed in time, once the Union won the war.) And as long as Northern troops were kept out of the South, it couldn't really set anyone free there, either.

Yet Lincoln's proclamation had a great effect. News of it spread behind enemy lines to the plantations of the South. Slaves who were able to escape ran off by the thousands and joined the Union armies to fight for the freedom of those slaves they'd left behind.

Then the South began winning again—and once more General Lee's Confederate forces invaded the North. Sweeping past Washington, they pushed all the way through Maryland into Pennsylvania.

The news that Lee was heading for Harrisburg and Philadelphia spread panic throughout the North. In the great southern battles of Richmond, Manassas, Fredericksburg, and Chancellorsville, he had already defeated the Union's Army of the Potomac. Now the unbeatable general was on Union territory!

Lee's forces were moving so fast that no one quite knew where they were. Lincoln gave orders to find them and stop them. And the two armies met almost by accident just outside a little town called Gettysburg.

Once the battle started, it raged on for three days. On the third day Lee sent fifteen thousand troops charging straight up a hill called Cemetery Ridge.

The fire from Union rifles and big guns mowed down half the Confederate soldiers before they ever reached the top of the hill. Those that made it as far as the Union lines had to battle hand to hand with Union soldiers. Bayonets flashed in the air. Rifles were used as clubs.

Over fifty thousand soldiers were killed or wounded at Gettysburg. Never before in this country's history had so many Americans been lost in a single battle. But General Lee's army had been stopped. His attempt to win the war by invading the North was over.

Lee led his dazed and bleeding troops back to the South. From this point on, the North grew increasingly stronger. On July 4, 1863, the last day of the battle at Gettysburg, General Ulysses S. Grant led the Union forces in taking Vicksburg, Mississippi. In this way the union gained control of the Mississippi River.

These events marked a turning point in the war. Abe traveled to the battlefield at Gettysburg to speak to the nation. It was there that he delivered his famous Gettysburg Address on November 19, 1863.

"Fourscore and seven years ago," he began by saying, "our fathers brought forth on this continent a new nation, conceived in liberty, and dedicated to the proposition that all men are created equal." He talked about the "honored dead" who gave their "last full measure of devotion" in fighting for that cause. And he ended by asking the American people to "here highly resolve that these dead shall not have

died in vain—that this nation, under God, shall have a new birth of freedom—and that government of the people, by the people, for the people, shall not perish from the earth."

Lincoln's address at Gettysburg was spoken from the heart—but he was still filled with great sadness. There were times when he felt so bad about all the killing that he could hardly bear it. Generals worried when he showed up in his tall hat in the midst of battle and would not duck his head.

But Lincoln must have wanted to be strong for the frightened young men who were fighting these battles and their just as frightened loved ones back home.

One Nation

The fierce struggle dragged on for almost two more years before Northern armies under General Grant and General William T. Sherman marched into the South. Though losing, the weakened South fought on. Finally on April 9, 1865, at Appomattox Court House in Virginia, General Lee surrendered to General Grant. At last the bloody Civil War was over.

But how should the South be treated now that the war had ended? Abe thought that there had been too much suffering already. To take revenge upon anyone now would only mean that Americans were still hurting Americans. Punishing the South would keep hatred alive. That was why he asked the people to show "malice towards none" and "charity for all."

Now Abe gave orders to allow Confederate soldiers to keep their horses. Abe knew from a childhood of living on farms that these men would need their animals to pull the plows on the farms that they had neglected for so long.

Despite Lincoln's great mercy, he was not loved by all. People living in the North who had sided with the Confederacy were called Copperheads. They had hated Abe during the war—and when the South was defeated, they hated him all the more.

Abe was worried. Five days after Lee's surrender he said to a man who was guarding him, "Do you know, I believe there are men who want to take my life." He grew thoughtful for a moment, then he added, "And I have no doubt they will do it."

On that same evening he and Mrs. Lincoln went to see a play at Ford's Theatre in Washington. It was a comedy called *Our American Cousin*, just the thing to help him relax.

After arriving late, the Lincolns went up a staircase to a special box on the balcony. No one, not even their guard, noticed the little peephole that had just been drilled in the door to the box. The man who had done this was an actor named John Wilkes Booth. Booth wasn't in the play, but he often collected his mail at the theater. He had learned the day before that the President would be coming and immediately set his assassination plan in motion. There were other men involved in the plot, too. One of them was supposed to kill the Vice President, and a third had the job of murdering the Secretary of State.

But Booth wanted the "glory" of assassinating Abraham Lincoln. He got his chance when the President's bodyguard became so interested in the play that he left his post by the box door and went off to watch the play. Quickly Booth went up to the balcony and looked through the peephole. As soon as he saw where Abe was sitting, Booth opened the door, stepped into the box, and fired his revolver.

The other victims of the plot escaped death. Secretary Seward and four others in his home were stabbed by a ferocious attacker, but they recovered. The man who planned to shoot Vice President Andrew Johnson grew frightened and ran off.

Abraham Lincoln was carried to a house across the street from the theater. Mary Lincoln begged the doctor to save her husband. But the President died early the next morning, and America was sick at heart. In great cities and tiny villages of the North, bells were rung to mourn this great man who had preserved the Union in its darkest moments.

Rather than bury Abe in Washington, Mrs. Lincoln wanted to bring her husband's body home to Springfield, Illinois. He was placed inside a seven-car funeral train. The first stop was Baltimore, where Abe was once so hated he had to be smuggled through the city. But now people came by the thousands to mourn him. The train slowly continued its journey west, stopping at big cities, where his coffin was taken off the train so that the people could see him for one last time. In the countryside people lined the tracks and gathered at the railroad stations. Old and young alike came to bid farewell to their beloved President.

Abe's funeral train rolled through the North, but in the South the newly freed slaves also mourned for the Great Emancipator. Even Abe's wartime enemy, General Robert E. Lee, grieved when he heard of the murder. He believed Lincoln's death to be a terrible blow to the South. When he surrendered his troops, he'd counted on the mercy of the President toward the people of the defeated Confederacy.

There were other Southerners who agreed with their general. They had lost the war and could not defend themselves. Many of their cities, plantations, and farms had been destroyed or burned to the ground. Abe Lincoln might have helped them rebuild. He might have protected them from those who wanted to take revenge. But the man who had said, "With malice towards none; with charity for all" was gone.

Abe's dream of completely ending slavery in this country came true on December 18, 1865, when the Thirteenth Amendment to the Constitution was passed. His profound words will always be remembered: "In *giving* freedom to the *slave*, we *assure* freedom to the *free*."

But the Thirteenth Amendment did not guarantee equality for all people. That struggle has gone on for more than one hundred years since Abe's death—and it continues today.

Abraham Lincoln is a symbol of that struggle. We have erected a monument to honor him, the Lincoln Memorial in Washington, D.C. We have named places and schools after him, and we celebrate his birthday.

We have done this so that we can always remember what he stood for—a government of the people, by the people, and for the people.

Lincoln's Address at Gettysburg, 1863

Fourscore and seven years ago our fathers brought forth on this continent a new nation, conceived in Liberty, and dedicated to the proposition that all men are created equal.

Now we are engaged in a great civil war, testing whether that nation or any nation so conceived and so dedicated can long endure. We are met on a great battlefield of that war. We have come to dedicate a portion of that field as a final resting place for those who here gave their lives that that nation might live. It is altogether fitting and proper that we should do this.

But in a larger sense we cannot dedicate—we cannot consecrate—we cannot hallow—this ground. The brave men, living and dead, who struggled here, have consecrated it, far above our poor power to add or detract. The world will little note nor long remember what we say here, but it can never forget what they did here. It is for us the living, rather, to be dedicated here to the unfinished work which they who fought here have thus far so nobly advanced. It is rather for us to be here dedicated to the great task remaining before us—that from these honored dead we take increased devotion to that cause for which they gave the last full measure of devotion—that we here highly resolve that these dead shall not have died in vain—that this nation, under God, shall have a new birth of freedom—and that government of the people, by the people, for the people, shall not perish from the earth.

Highlights in the Life of
ABRAHAM LINCOLN

1809   Abraham Lincoln is born on February 12 in a log cabin in the Kentucky wilderness.

1816   The Lincoln family moves to a new farm in southern Indiana and lives through winter in an open shed.

1818   Abe's mother, Nancy Hanks Lincoln, dies of the "milk sick."

1820   Abe's father, having married Sarah Bush Johnson, brings her and her three children to live with Abe, Sarah, and their cousin Dennis Hanks.

1828   Working as a boatman, Abe makes his first trip down the Mississippi

River to New Orleans, the center of the slave trade.

1830   Abe moves with his family to Illinois.

1831   Abe makes his second flatboat trip to New Orleans and vows to fight slavery.

1832   Abe serves as captain in the Black Hawk War.

1834   Abe is elected to the Illinois State Legislature and soon becomes one of the Whig party leaders.

1837   Abe becomes a lawyer and practices in Springfield.

1842   Abe marries Mary Todd.

1846   Abe is elected to Congress. He proposes that slave owners in the District of Columbia be paid to set their slaves free. He also loses popularity back home by saying that the war against Mexico is unconstitutional and was unjustly started by the United States.

1854 Senator Douglas's Kansas-Nebraska Act overthrows the Missouri Compromise. This opens the northwestern territories to slavery.

1857 In its Dred Scott decision, the Supreme Court decides that a slave cannot sue for his freedom, because he is only "property." The court also declares that no free Negro may become a citizen of the United States and that laws enacted to keep slavery out of any state are unconstitutional.

1858 Lincoln and Douglas debate each other over the expansion of slavery into the territories.

1859 John Brown attempts to start a slave rebellion in the South by leading an attack on a government arsenal at Harper's Ferry. He is captured and later hanged.

1860	Lincoln is elected President of the United States on November 6.
1860	In December South Carolina is the first state to secede from the Union. Others soon follow.
1861	Fort Sumter is fired upon on April 14, and the Civil War begins.
1863	Lincoln signs the Emancipation Proclamation on January 1.
1863	General Robert E. Lee's army is defeated at Gettysburg on July 4. From then on, the South starts to lose the war.
1863	Lincoln delivers the Gettysburg Address on November 19.
1865	On April 9 General Lee surrenders to General Ulysses S. Grant at Appomattox Court House in Virginia, ending the Civil War.
1865	On April 14 Lincoln is assassinated by actor John Wilkes Booth at Ford's Theatre in Washington, D.C.